JUKEBOX

Dieter Ladwig

CHARTWELL
BOOKS, INC.

INTRODUCTION

If you've been collecting jukeboxes with greater or lesser degrees of enthusiasm for the past 20 years, writing a book about them would seem to be the next logical step. Obviously this particular book is written very much from a collector's point of view. But I have also tried to describe some of the long and complex history of the jukebox, from the time Edison effectively "invented" it, through the time I saw my first AMI H 200 music box at the age of 15 in 1957, to the present day. I owe a huge debt of thanks to my many friends and acquaintances all over the world who have helped me obtain jukeboxes and spare parts; to my former girlfriends Ulla, Bianca and Sylvia, my restorer Rolf and my parents, who were the first to diagnose and give a name to my condition: Jukebox Crazy. Thanks are due also to Mr. Jordan, the only person able to help me solve a variety of technical problems, and to big brother Fred for the flights around the world.

Translated by Phil Goddard
in association with First Edition Translations, Cambridge, UK
Photography by the author

Published by
CHARTWELL BOOKS, INC.
A Division of **BOOK SALES, INC.**
110 Enterprise Avenue
Secaucus. New Jersey 07094

CLB 4095
© 1994 this English language edition CLB Publishing, Godalming, Surrey, England
Originally published in German by V.I.P.
© 1992 Paul Zsolnay Verlag Ges.m.b.H, Vienna
Printed in Italy
ISBN 0-7858-0080-8

THE HISTORY OF THE JUKEBOX

When Thomas Alva Edison was working away in his laboratory in 1871, he could never have dreamed of the uses to which his discoveries would one day be put. His main concern was to improve the Morse apparatus and develop his own telegraph machine, but in passing he discovered that he could use a machine to reproduce the sound of the human voice. This discovery banished all thoughts of a telegraph from his mind, and instead he began making his own phonograph, based on a wax cylinder which would be used to store and reproduce sound. Edison developed some 1,400 inventions during his career, and he sold the patent to this one for $10,000 in cash. As is so often the case, the man who invented the machine benefited the least, and large numbers of people subsequently made a great deal of money out of it. Edison then went on to invent the lightbulb.

The next step in the history of the jukebox occurred in Germany in 1887, when Emil Berliner patented the gramophone. It was now only a matter of time until the phonograph was used for recording and playing music, and in fact the first coin-operated phonographs appeared in San Francisco before 1900. Louis Glass set up the first machines in 1889 in the Palais Royal Saloon: these had two earpieces and cost 20 cents to operate, which had to be paid by each person listening. Company reports from the time show that these machines made a huge profit of up to $2,000 in only two months.

With so much money at stake, it was inevitable that the market would soon be flooded with bootlegged records and other forms of musical piracy. The phonograph manufacturers charged around 50 percent of the annual takings, which averaged around $5,000: again this was a huge profit when the machines cost only $100 or so to make.

As people realized how profitable jukeboxes were, many new companies sprang up, only to disappear almost as quickly. Phonograph Arcades began to be set up in Europe and the US, one example being the Pathé Salon du Phonographie in Paris. These contained rows of coin-operated phonographs where people could make their own choice of music: the machines even had cloths hanging from them to clean the earpiece. In some of these arcades, it was possible to hear up to 1,000 pieces of music: the staff playing the selected pieces were hidden behind the wall hangings. Increasingly, phonographs were installed in other public places such as restaurants, where they had large horn-shaped loudspeakers which enabled more customers to hear the music. With recording technology still in its infancy, the music they heard was noisy and scratchy.

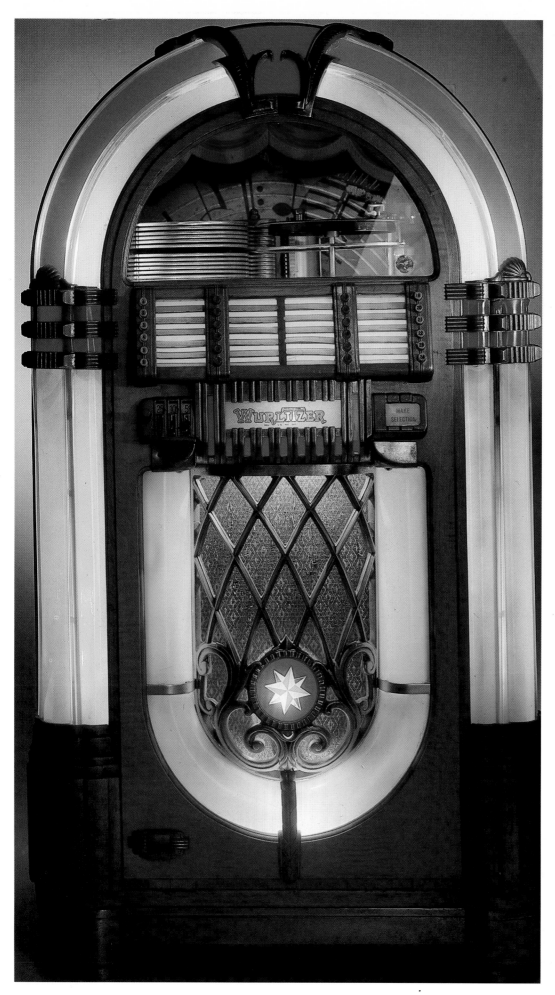

The Wurlitzer 1015: the classic jukebox which is every collector's dream. The 1015 was the biggest-selling jukebox of all time, partly because it had the biggest sales campaign of all time and partly due to the brilliant design by Paul Fuller. Its combination of plastic, die-cast zinc and wood made it easily the most attractive of all machines from the golden age of the jukebox. The rotating, four-colored cylinders on either side produced constantly changing combinations of yellow, violet, red and green. The eight bubble tunes at the top and side added to the effect, with liquid being heated to produce a flow of bubbles. Around 56,000 of these machines were sold in 1946-47. The 1015 contained twenty-four 78 rpm records which were playable only on one side, although other manufacturers such as AMI were already incorporating 24 double-sided records. But even at this early stage, Wurlitzer was synonymous with jukeboxes.

A Wurlitzer machine in the author's restaurant in Düsseldorf, Germany: Dee's American Diner. Jukeboxes were an essential feature of these diners, which were often made from redundant railroad cars and provided American-style fast food.

The first direct forerunner of the jukebox was produced by the manufacturer Gabel in 1906. This allowed individual records to be selected and listened to through a horn-shaped loudspeaker, but this machine had technical problems and production was soon halted. Also, the reproduction quality of radio was improving, and it was starting to become a serious competitor to the phonograph. But manufacturers stayed one step ahead, by introducing many new features to phonographs and laying the foundations of a large-scale industry. In 1927, the introduction of the electric amplifier meant that a jukebox could compete with a big band for the first time.

The high point for jukeboxes came after the Second World War, as Americans increasingly made their decisions about where to go on a Saturday night based on the quality of the jukebox. Only the best bars and restaurants could afford live jazz and dance bands, and in many others the center of the entertainment was the jukebox. The most successful and popular machine was designed for Wurlitzer by Paul Fuller, who produced the extraordinary 1015, with its dazzling display of chrome, fluorescent tubes and color. Some 56,000 of these machines were sold within a short space of time.

The jukebox era ended around 1948, as the public became increasingly domesticated. The manufacturer Mills disappeared from the market, and Wurlitzer sold only 7,000 of its 1100 model.

The beginning of the conservative 1950s also saw the appearance of the small, much less fragile 45 rpm record. Jukeboxes had been playing heavyweight 78s for the past 40 years, and there were no machines for playing 45s until Seeburg brought out one which offered a choice of 100 tracks in 1948. This machine was also equipped to take 78s and could easily be converted. The new machine, the M 100 A, had a wholly new design.

In the 1970s, the jukebox acquired a new popularity with the advent of rock music: jukeboxes playing rock became the expression of an age. There had been a slump in interest in jukeboxes in the 1960s with the arrival of the discotheque, and records had also become better and cheaper so that people could buy music for themselves. The big manufacturers suffered serious losses: AMI merged with another company, and in the United States, Wurlitzer shut down its American operation in 1974. In Germany, Wurlitzer had started separate production in 1960, and along with NSM/Löwen it is the only significant company in the country. Both companies now export machines to the United States.

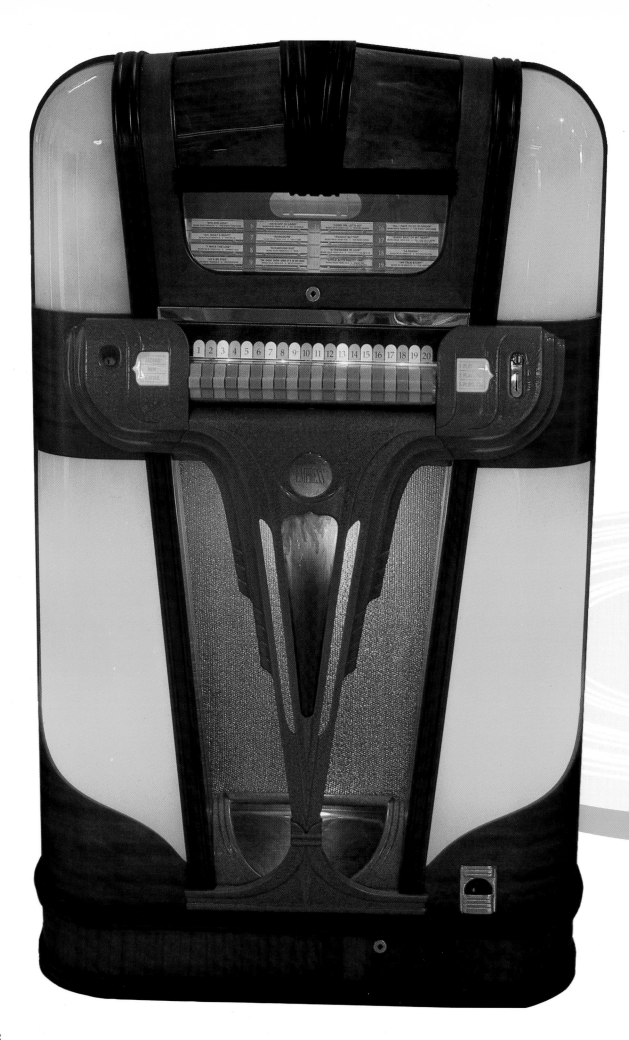

A very rare and attractive Mills "Empress" dating from 1939. Its unusual features include an Art Deco design and a concealed changer mechanism holding 20 records.

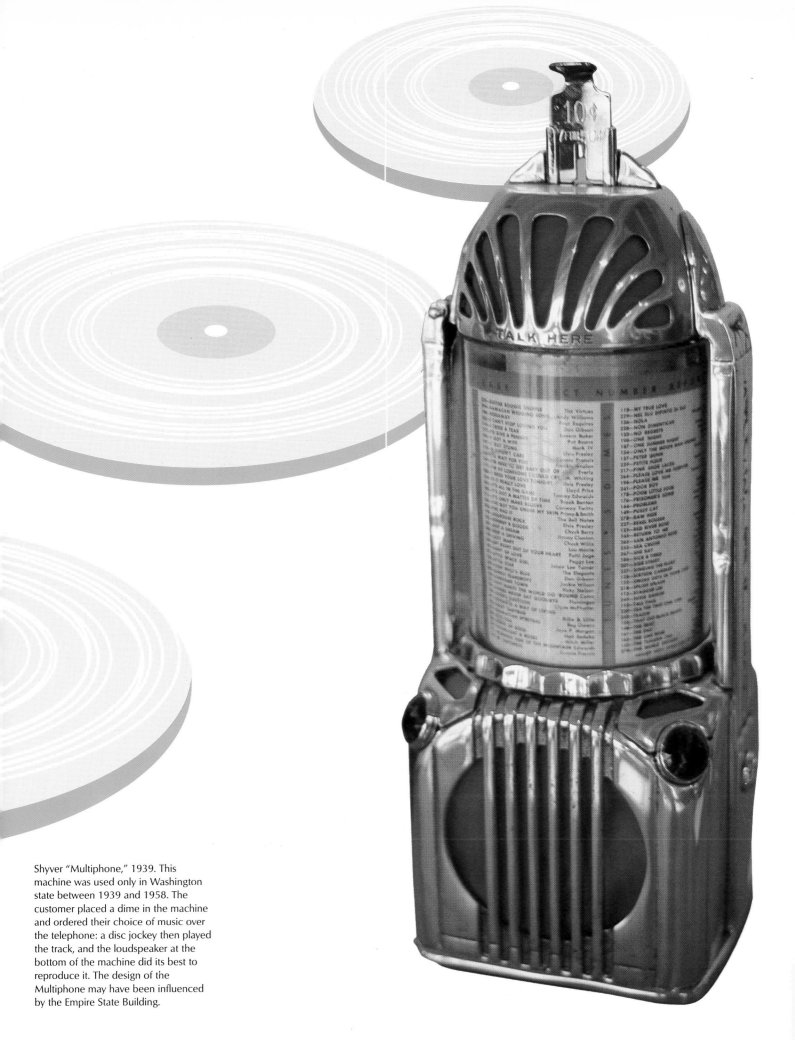

Shyver "Multiphone," 1939. This machine was used only in Washington state between 1939 and 1958. The customer placed a dime in the machine and ordered their choice of music over the telephone: a disc jockey then played the track, and the loudspeaker at the bottom of the machine did its best to reproduce it. The design of the Multiphone may have been influenced by the Empire State Building.

Mills "Throne of Music," 1939. This was a very similar machine to the "Empress" of the same year.

1938 Wurlitzer 500. This machine had a more rounded and attractive outline than its more angular predecessors, as well as a new keyboard selector and revolving colored cylinders, with a wood veneer cabinet. It was highly decorative and sold well at trade exhibitions at the time.

This AMI "Model 201 Singing Tower" (1940) bears a strong and probably deliberate resemblance to a skyscraper. This box was the first to have a record changer which played both sides of ten records. This was a major technical advance, especially as the market leader, Wurlitzer, did not introduce this mechanism for another ten years. With the exception of the red plastics of the selector, all the transparent parts of the machine were made from very thick glass. The center is made from mirror glass and the body of metal. The attractive top dome was designed to broadcast the music in all directions.

AMI "Model Singing Tower" (1940), a beautifully designed and colored jukebox full of lovingly crafted detail.

Wurlitzer "Counter Model 71," 1941. These
machines, also known as table models, for a long
time provided an alternative to the full-size
jukebox in locations where there was limited
space. However, they could play only 12 records.
This and the Model 81 were among the most
attractive of their time, and around 4,500 were
made in 1940 and 1941. There is also an 810
Counter Model Stand for this box: this was a
slightly rounded column inlaid with wood, which
is now very rare.

Seeburg "Concert Master," 1940. This has a highly unusual design featuring two masks representing tragedy and comedy. I think this is one of the finest of all Seeburgs, with its body painted in warm marble tones, red and blue plastics and metal ornamentation: definitely one of the outstanding models of its time.

Wurlitzer 700, dating from 1940. A total of 9,500 of these machines, designed by Paul Fuller, were sold. A Wurlitzer brochure of the time claims that the multi-colored pillars are made of costly Italian onyx; they are actually made of brightly colored plastic. The design also incorporated red, yellow and green plastic panels. It played only 24 records, but with artists like Bing Crosby, Glenn Miller and Benny Goodman, who was complaining?

1941 Wurlitzer 750:
one of the most
attractive jukeboxes
of all time. This
featured two arched
bubble tubes on
either side of the
coin slot (which took
nickels, dimes and
quarters), and was a
much smaller model
than many of its
contemporaries.
People clearly
appreciated the
design by Paul Fuller:
a total of 18,000
were sold.

1941 Wurlitzer 780. Like the 1080 model of 1947, this box was described as a Colonial model and had an almost cathedral-like solemnity which failed to deter 3,500 people from buying it. The decoration at the bottom is clearly a spinning wheel, but collectors call this jukebox the "Wagon Wheel." The spinning wheel, patchwork design and old-fashioned wooden structure were designed to create a cosy, homely atmosphere.

1941 Wurlitzer 850, known by collectors as the "Peacock." Many enthusiasts believe it is Paul Fuller's finest piece of work. The two Art Nouveau peacocks in the middle change color constantly as a disc rotates behind them; the bubble tubes are surrounded by metal scrolls and the grille is overlaid with gold brocade. Bright green plastics inside the machine and nickel-plated metal edging complete the picture.

Wurlitzer "Counter Model 41," 1941. A beautifully restored machine with 12 records.

Seeburg "Top Spot," 1941. The speaker, originally designed for the "Concert Master," with its symbolic organ pipes and two masks, have made it a rare and greatly sought-after collector's piece.

Wurlitzer 950, a Victory model dating from 1942. Collectors regard it as the finest jukebox of all time, but only 3,400 were ever built. Wartime materials shortages meant that the box was made almost wholly of wood: this was the first machine to feature long bubble tubes in the side pillars. The leaping gazelles in the grille constantly changed color.

Rock-Ola "Commando," 1942.
This was another machine made
in wartime when materials were
scarce, but of great beauty
nevertheless. The illuminated
upper part was made of glass
rather than plastic.

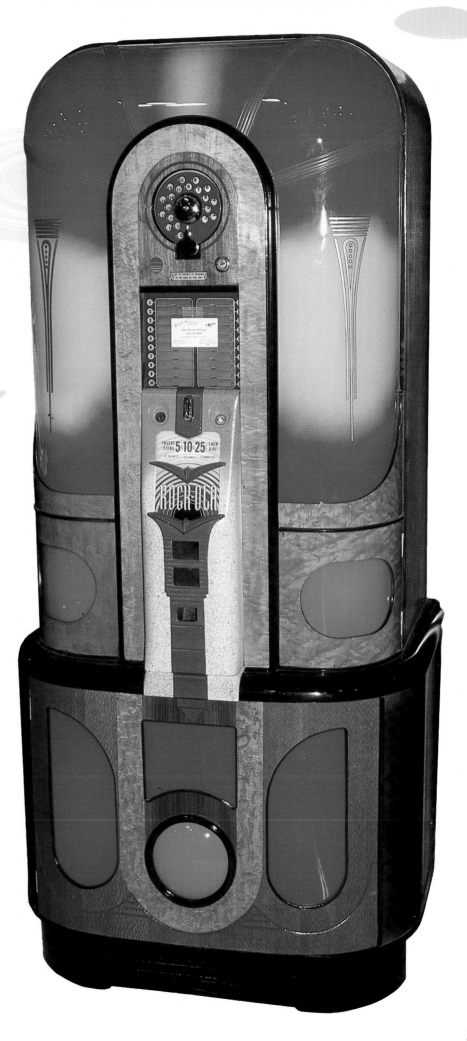

Wurlitzer "Model 42,"
1942. A distinctly
unusual and highly
decorative design;
like others of its time it
was known as
a Victory model.
It contained little
metal and no plastic,
and could be fitted
as an empty shell
over another,
older machine.

AMI "A," 1946. Known as Mother of Plastic for its mother-of-pearl effect, and the first jukebox to use acrylic, 11,200 of these machines were sold in two years. The machine played both sides of 20 records, which was a major technical improvement.

Packard "Pla-Mor," an "economy model" from 1946, with very deep-set plastics, designed by Homer E. Capehart. The "Pla-Mor" played 24 titles.

Wurlitzer's advertisement for the 1015 (1947)

Advertisement for the Wurlitzer Model 1080 from the same year

Seeburg S 148, 1948
Appropriately nicknamed the "washing machine," "barrel" and "trashcan," it was nevertheless an objec of considerable beauty, one of the most original and rarest of all Seeburg machines. The revolving colored cylinders in the dome and the lower part of the grille distinguish it from the S 146 and S 147. It plays 20 different 78 rpm records, and the mechanism is unusually reliable.

THE BIG NAMES

WURLITZER

Rudolph Wurlitzer Company, North Tokawanda, New York.
A famous name in music for over a
hundred years.

Wurlitzer "Colonial 1080," 1947. A masterpiece of elaborate old-world charm in the Colonial style, its grille decorated with the early American lyre. Some 7,000 of these machines were made, often for locations where they needed to blend into the background. The tone arm is a huge metal monster on the right-hand side.

Detail of the "Colonial 1080"

The German craftsman Rudolph Wurlitzer emigrated to America in 1853. He began working in a variety of casual jobs, but gradually began using his skills to make musical instruments. He started dealing in instruments imported from Germany, and made money out of the Civil War by supplying them to the marching bands of the Union forces. By the end of the war, Wurlitzer was the country's biggest manufacturer of band instruments.

But Wurlitzer was also becoming interested in nickel-in-a-slot phonographs. It was from this interest that the famous Wurlitzer organs derived, including the Mighty Wurlitzer which was used to accompany silent movies.

Rudolph Wurlitzer died in 1914, but the company continued to flourish under his third son, Farny. By 1920 it had achieved sales of several million dollars a year. The company suffered major problems as a result of the Wall Street Crash, but after the Recession had ended it became the market leader again. The number of potential locations for jukeboxes was also growing steadily, and an instruction manual for salesmen selling Wurlitzer Counter Model 71s lists all the conceivable places where one could be located; only bathrooms were missing from the list. The salesmen were certainly successful.

The company's real rise to fame began in the 1930s, when Farny Wurlitzer met Homer E. Capehart, a brilliant salesman who made his own phonographs. He was in search of new financial backing after a financial collapse and therefore sold first his distribution rights, and then his own services, to Wurlitzer. A few years later he was managing the company's jukebox division, and in 1934 large-scale production began with the "P 10-Simplex." This had a wooden case and a telephone selector dial with 12 titles. Capehart promised he would sell around 25,000 of these machines by 1935. In 1936, sales had already reached 65,000.

Wurlitzer's other major rivals, such as Seeburg, AMI and Mills, were selling only a fifth of this figure and, thanks to Capehart's genius at salesmanship, Wurlitzer achieved a net profit of around $500,000 in 1936. By 1937 it had established a market share of almost 50 percent, but the market was rapidly approaching saturation point. This was to result in far more aggressive competition, with each company operating its own sales strategy. Wurlitzer's sales fell by 25 percent, and Capehart left the business in 1940. But he had created a milestone in the history of the jukebox business, and said later in an interview that although other people had made jukeboxes, he had shown them how it was done.

The greatest Wurlitzer jukeboxes were designed by Paul Fuller between 1934 and 1948: Fuller had the knack of making his machines look highly attractive. Although the mechanism hardly changed, Wurlitzer launched up to seven new designs each year.

ROCK-OLA

David C. Rockola was another of the four giants
of the jukebox world.

Rock-Ola 1426 (1947).
This was the successor to
the 1422, and included only
minor changes. It has two
illuminated colored
cylinders, a metal grille
and a gold-colored
background decorated with
two jewel-encrusted mirrors.

Detail of the Rock-Ola "1426"

Despite appearances, the name of this company had nothing to do with rock and roll: this was actually the family name of its owner, who came from Manitoba in Canada. Like Wurlitzer, Rockola did casual work before leaving for the States when he was about 20, where he went into partnership repairing and selling weighing scales for stores. In 1926 he began manufacturing his own, and also began investing in the new pinball business during the 1930s.

At first Rockola suffered a number of major financial setbacks before eventually getting his company onto an even keel. Very soon he was one of the country's biggest pinball manufacturers, and started exploring other areas of the slot machine business. In the mid-1930s he acquired the rights to a jukebox mechanism, which he then went on to improve.

As the prospects for the pinball business were uncertain, with many states banning it as a form of gambling, Rockola decided to set up a separate arm of the business making jukeboxes. He met with considerable hostility from Wurlitzer, which tried to keep him out of the market first by negotiation and offers of joint projects and later, when these were unsuccessful, with lawsuits for breaches of patent. Rockola had to find several hundred thousand dollars in court costs, but despite all this adversity he managed to establish a niche for his company in this hotly contested business. He was helped considerably by David C. Kochole, who designed a large number of beautiful jukeboxes for him.

Wurlitzer 1100 (1948). Sadly, this machine marked the end of the golden age of jukeboxes. Collectors describe the period which followed as the "silver age," but it was not the same. The 100 was the last great masterpiece bequeathed to the world by Paul Fuller, who is believed to have been influenced by the design of the American air force's B17-F Flying Fortress bomber; hence one of the nicknames given to this machine, the "Bomber Nose." Because of its Gothic cathedral shape, it was also known as the "Chapel," and as the "Bullet." The machine was based on the successful 1015, but despite making 16,000 of them, Wurlitzer managed to sell only 7,000. This was probably because the Seeburg M 100 A was technically superior.

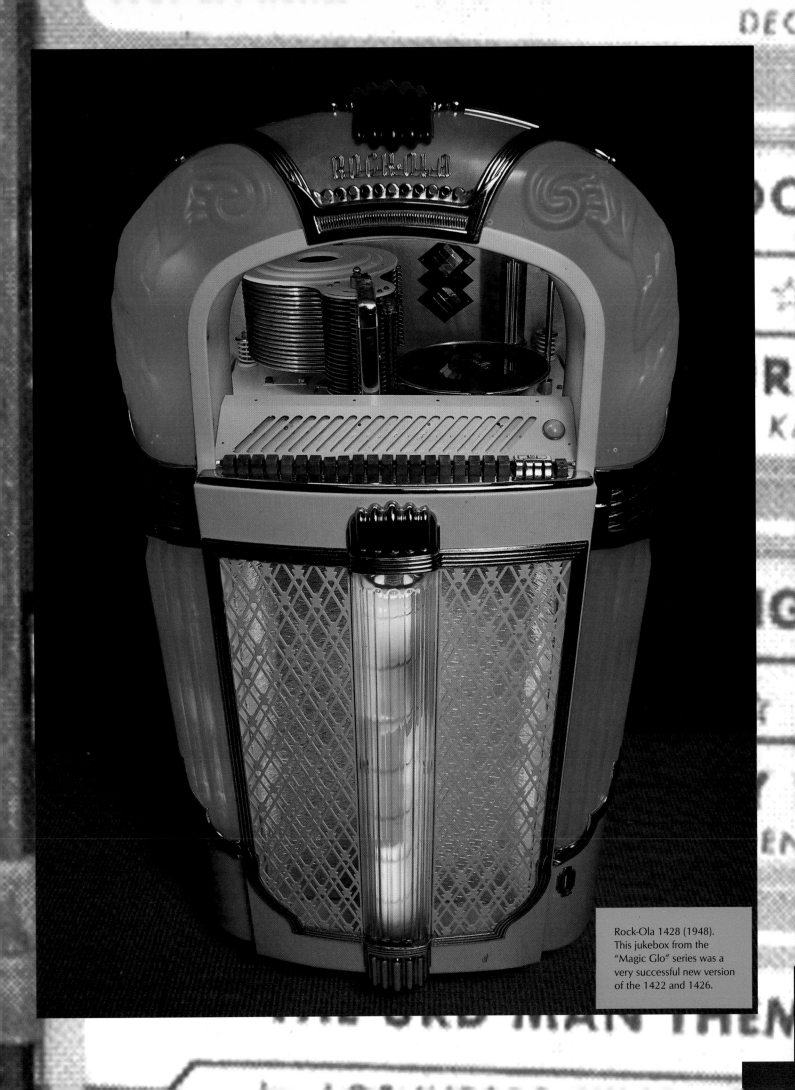

Rock-Ola 1428 (1948). This jukebox from the "Magic Glo" series was a very successful new version of the 1422 and 1426.

SEEBURG

Like Wurlitzer and Rockola, Justus P. Seeburg was a
relatively recent immigrant, in this case
from Gothenburg in Sweden.

Seeburg "Teardrop" loudspeaker from the 1940s

In 1886, at the age of 16, Seeburg left Sweden and found a job with the Piano Company in Chicago. Here, he became well versed in the workings of automatic musical instruments. In 1906 he set up his own company, realizing that there was a great deal of money to be made from manufacturing and installing these machines. Like Capehart at Wurlitzer, Seeburg was a very good salesman. He began by making orchestrions: mechanical pianos which were accompanied by other automatic instruments. He also realized the potential profits to be made from the phonograph, and so began experimenting with a record changer mechanism.

Seeburg spent nearly eight years building Audiophones, a range of very large jukeboxes. The company suffered a number of setbacks as a result of lost production caused by the Wall Street Crash, and a series of jukeboxes which suffered from technical problems. But over the years that followed, the company produced a number of very fine jukeboxes, including the "Classic," the 9800, the "Envoy" and the "Symphola." In terms both of their design and their technical features, Seeburg produced far better jukeboxes than its competitors. In 1938, Seeburg introduced the first illuminated jukebox. Designed by Nils Miller, the outside of the machine was clad in transparent plastic, an innovation which was immediately copied by Seeburg's rivals. Apart from the "Light Up Symphola," there were also accessories for older jukeboxes such as the "Dome" which enabled lighting to be built in subsequently.

At the same time, the company was also producing the "Wall-o-matic" and the "Play-Boy." This innovation enabled records to be selected from customers' tables instead of having to go over to the jukebox. These machines offered a choice of about 20 tracks; in 1948 Seeburg produced the M 100 A, which played 100 records.

When he reached the age of 60, Seeburg handed the company over to his son Noel. Under his management, the company made a number of jukeboxes incorporating an unusually reliable record changer, which are still working well in many collectors' machines all these decades later.

33

CAPEHART

Homer E. Capehart also made his own jukeboxes before joining Wurlitzer. He began his career selling vending machines for chocolate, chewing gum and similar items, but then became increasingly interested in automatic musical instruments. Capehart bought a machine at his own expense and showed it to the owner of his company in the hope of gaining promotion: instead he was sacked for having the machine in his possession. Capehart then went on to make his own jukeboxes, and designed the first machine to play both sides of a record. However, this jukebox, the "Orchestrope," proved very unreliable in high temperatures, and also encountered patent problems. Capehart was forced to recall and repair the faulty machines. Although he survived both this and the Depression, and his machines sold well around the world, the market was highly competitive and his company eventually ran out of money.

Two Wurlitzers, a 700 and a 1080, adding a touch of nostalgia to an imitation of Rick's American Café from the film *Casablanca*.

MILLS, GABEL, FILBEN AND AMI

AMI "C" (1950)

The gaming machine manufacturer Mills also became involved in jukebox production at a very early stage. In 1906 it produced the "Virtuoso," which proved a sensation despite its poor sound quality. At first the founder of the company, Herbert Steven Mills, was not convinced that the jukebox had any business potential; he was only persuaded when his brother secretly built one and then showed him the finished product. Later, in 1926, Mills produced its first jukebox proper, the "Dance Master." Although Mills never became one of the really big manufacturers, two of its machines, the "Empress" and the "Throne of Music" (both 1939) became classics of Art Deco design. Eventually, the founder's misgivings were proved right: one of Mills' postwar machines, the "Constellation" was a total flop, and the company made a number of other mistakes which eventually led to its being declared bankrupt in 1948: its value had slumped from around $10 million in 1940 to only $50,000 when it went out of business.

Apart from the major manufacturers, there were two other companies, Gabel and Filben, which produced a few successful jukeboxes: Filben's "Maestro" (1946) in particular was a visual masterpiece.

AMI, the Automatic Musical Instruments Company, also produced a large number of attractive jukeboxes which are still very popular with collectors. But, like the "Singing Tower" from the 1930s, these could hardly be called a commercial success. One unusual machine was the 1939 "Automatic Hostess," which used a telephone selection system. The selection was acknowledged by a female voice, and the machine then played the track, first greeting listeners if required.

Rock-Ola "Spectravox" Model 1802, dating from 1901. It was designed to be relatively inconspicuous, and could only be operated in conjunction with the Rock-Ola "Playmaster." It was described as a "hide away box;" the mechanism was not visible, and the machine usually stood in a corner of the dance floor.

Seeburg M 100 C
(1952). This model
was the last in
Seeburg's "M" series.

Rock-Ola 1434 (1951).
This jukebox, also known
as "Super Rocket,"
marked the end of the 78.
The 1434 was still
available with 50 78 rpm
selections, but was also
sold with 120 45s. The
following model, the
1436, played only 45s.

Wurlitzer "Model 81," the successor to the 71. The only visible difference was the dark, marble-colored side plastics; apart from these, the machine had the same design and the same mechanism. This machine is very rare and much sought after by collectors.

D

A Wurlitzer 1400 series from the 1950s, with a beautiful blue, silver and orange design featuring a South Sea paradise of canoes and palm trees. This machine could be used to play any record format, and another innovation was the inclusion of two tone arms so that records did not need to be turned over. However, this proved somewhat unreliable.

Bergmann "Symphonie 80" from the 1950s. This 40-record jukebox was fairly typical of its time, and certainly nothing to write home about.

AMI "Model D," 1951. "Music for you by AMI" announced this machine, which played 40 78 selections or 80 45s. The vinyl around the top of the machine was supposed to look like leather.

Filben "Maestro," 1946-1948: with its 30 selections,
this was Filben's only full-size box.

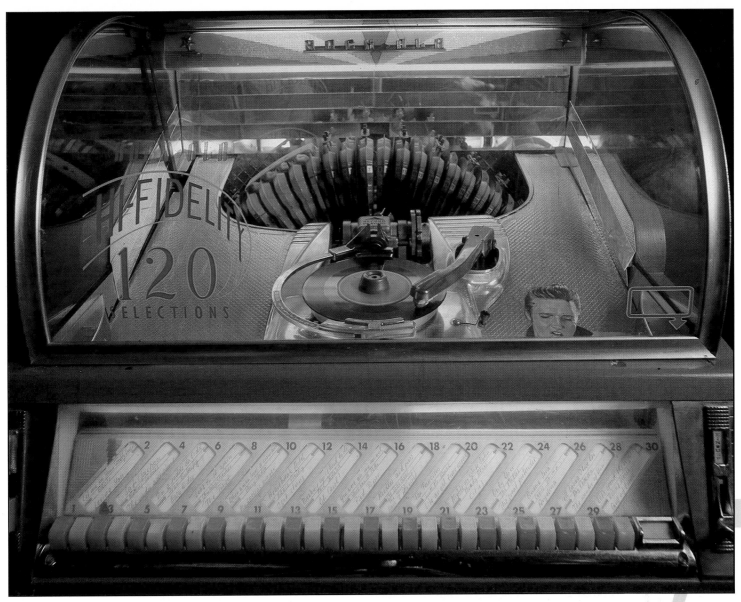

Detail of the "Comet 1446"

The Rock-Ola
"Comet 1446"
(1954), which
played 60 singles
and was described
as "high fidelity."

Wurlitzer 1250 (1950).
This jukebox had
48 selections and three
different record
formats. Wurlitzer
sold around 13,500.

Seeburg HF 100 R

A 1950s Wurlitzer 39A: another successful piece of loudspeaker design.

Rock-Ola 1442 (1954): described as "ideal for smaller locations," it offered only 25 singles to choose from.

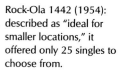

Wurlitzer "4008 Super de Luxe" from the 1940s. This ornately designed loudspeaker is identical to the top section of the Wurlitzer 1015 and was one of the best-selling models of its time.

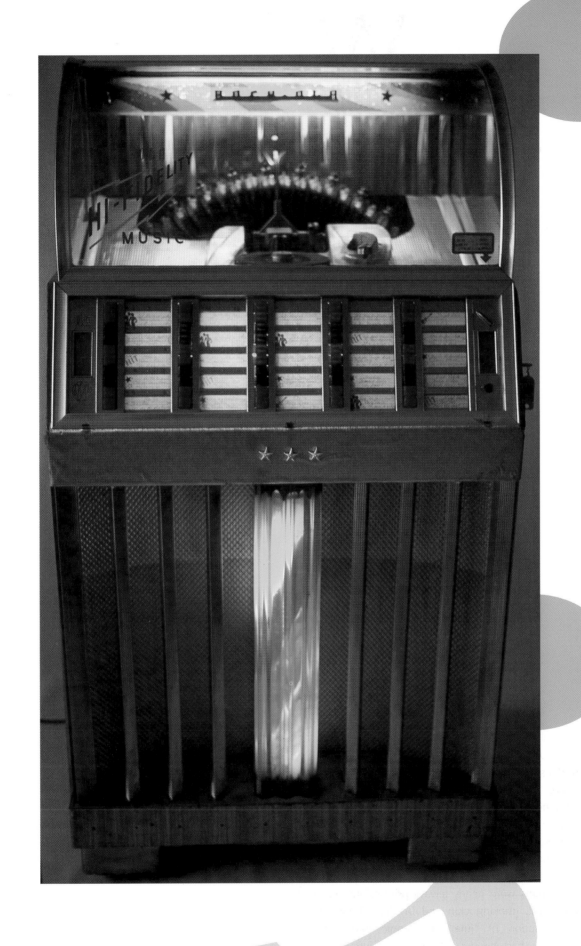

WHY "JUKEBOX?"

The word "juke" is believed to come from the southern United States, where a "juke joint" or "juke house" was a particular kind of meeting-place popular with black people.

In the 1920s, radio stations staged a boycott of black music: jazz, rhythm and blues were not publicly played, and slogans like "Stop! Help to save the youth of America! Don't buy negro records!" were common. But this discrimination was unable to suppress black music, and many believe that it was black artists who kept many record companies from going under during the Depression. Despite the boycott, black music was alive and well.

The word "juke" was synonymous with three things: dancing, music and sex. Juke joints were nearly always private, and were a mixture of dance hall, drinking club and brothel. The word may also be a corruption of "jute," as people frequented these places after they had been working in the jute fields. It was here that the inexorable rise of the jukebox – that most typical feature of American culture – began.

I saw my first jukebox when I was 15, but it was not until some 20 years later that I developed a real passion for them. When I heard my first Elvis record on my next-door neighbor's record player, it was a revelation, but this was placed in the shade by the discovery that the AMI H 200 jukebox of 1957, in my local bar, could play 100 of these records. Unfortunately I had little contact with jukeboxes for a long time after this, though as I grew older and my allowance increased, I was able to spend time and money listening to them.

Then my interest in jukeboxes received another setback as I discovered women. The beautiful AMI H 200 disappeared from the bar in the early 1960s, to be replaced by a really ugly machine. Although some technical enhancements were made to jukeboxes during the 1960s and '70s, there was very little improvement in terms of design.

It was around 20 years ago that my love affair with jukeboxes resumed. Somewhat better off than in my teenage years, I had the choice of going on holiday or buying a Wurlitzer 1450. After lengthy haggling over the price, I paid $2,400: the holiday was soon forgotten, and I became the proud owner of my very first jukebox.

I was now hopelessly addicted. I bought another one at a rather more affordable price, but I became so involved in the negotiations that the family Christmas went by the board. This in turn was followed by a Wurlitzer 1015, a Rock-Ola 1426 and a Wurlitzer 1100. Unfortunately, my girlfriend's interest in jukeboxes waned, as well it might: my relationship with her ended and was replaced by a long-term love affair with a machine. As very few jukeboxes were exported to my home country of Germany during the 1930s and '40s, I usually had to travel abroad to find them. I found some of the finest in southeast Asia, with varying degrees of difficulty. Once I traveled several hundred miles, and then walked a considerable distance, to view a Wurlitzer 1100 in the Philippines. When I got there, the owner refused to sell it.

The jukeboxes I bought were in very poor condition and it was doubtful whether they would ever be able to play records. So I went off in search of original parts which, although not difficult to get hold of, were expensive. One collector in the United States was charging $420 for a small red plastic part for a Rock-Ola 1428.

The problem of converting machines from 110 to 220 volts was solved relatively easily. Much more difficult was converting the drivewheel speed from the American 60 to the European 50 Hertz. A number of specialist electricians were unsuccessful, and the problem meant that Elvis Presley's "Blue Moon" was agony to listen to. Eventually, after a lot of phone calls, someone managed to make the new parts required and soon Elvis was singing away happily, but it had cost me $1,500 to convert a 1941 Wurlitzer 71.

If you're sufficiently addicted, high prices and problems in getting hold of machines and parts will not deter you from becoming a collector. Machines often appear on the market for the first time, and collectors are becoming increasingly interested in specific details of their technology or design. The passion for collecting jukeboxes is becoming more widespread, and it is not surprising that as an important product of American culture, jukeboxes are already finding their way into museums.

Top: Seeburg wall box from the 1950s. Unlike jukeboxes, the most attractive wall boxes were made in the 1950s. Earlier machines did not have the soft, rounded edges of these models, which allowed customers to select records from their table without having to go over to the jukebox itself.

Bottom: Seeburg wall box from the mid-1950s

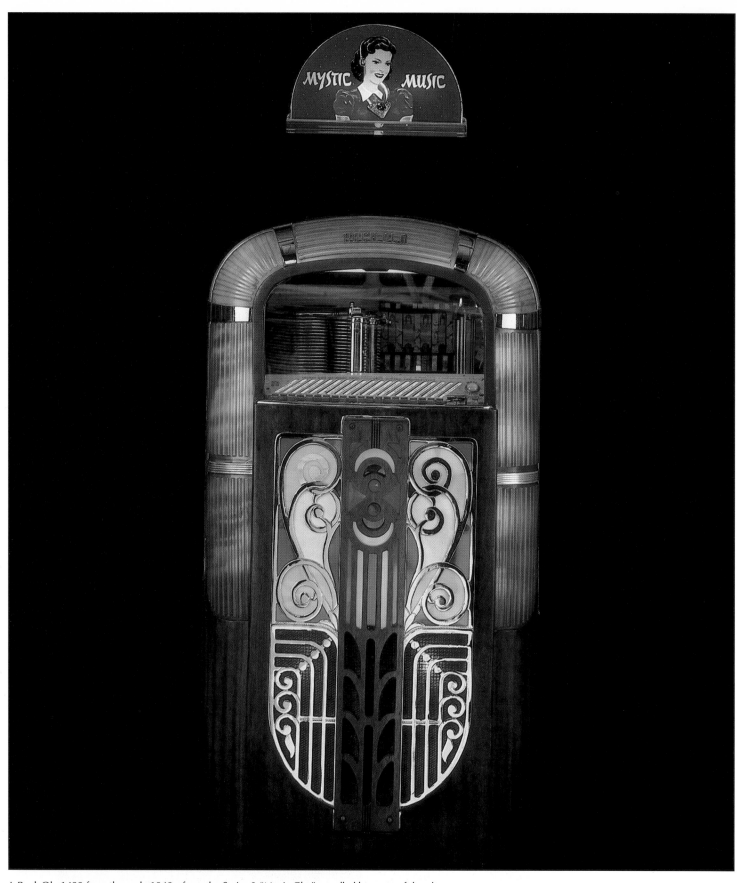

A Rock-Ola 1422 from the early 1940s, from the Series 3 "Magic Glo," so-called because of the glow emitted by the fluorescent tubes, lights and four colored cylinders. The center section is made of wood and the sides of the grille are metal.

An Arietta "Piccolo" from the 1950s. This has a very unusual mechanism, with the records arranged in a column and the tone arm moving up or down to the selected record.

A 1950s Bergmann "Symphonie 80," with an unusual design, like many British machines of the time. Minstrel's "Low Budget Box," for example, looked like a 1920s tank.

Wurlitzer 1800 from the 1950s. As the advertising put it, "the Model 1800 features the famous proven Wurlitzer Carousel Record Changer for trouble-free operation." This was certainly the case, and the machine is still very reliable.

Wurlitzer 1700 HF, a classic
from the 1950s

AMI "Model B" from the 50s: not as large as its predecessor, the Model A, but with a very attractively designed dome which emits a rotating colored light. The machine was available in two types of wood: "Sheraton mahogany" or "bisque blonde."

Rock-Ola "Comet Fireball 120 Model 1438," dating from 1954. This machine, with its two "color wheel plastic pilasters" trimmed with "tawny oak trimmed walnut," is much sought after among collectors.

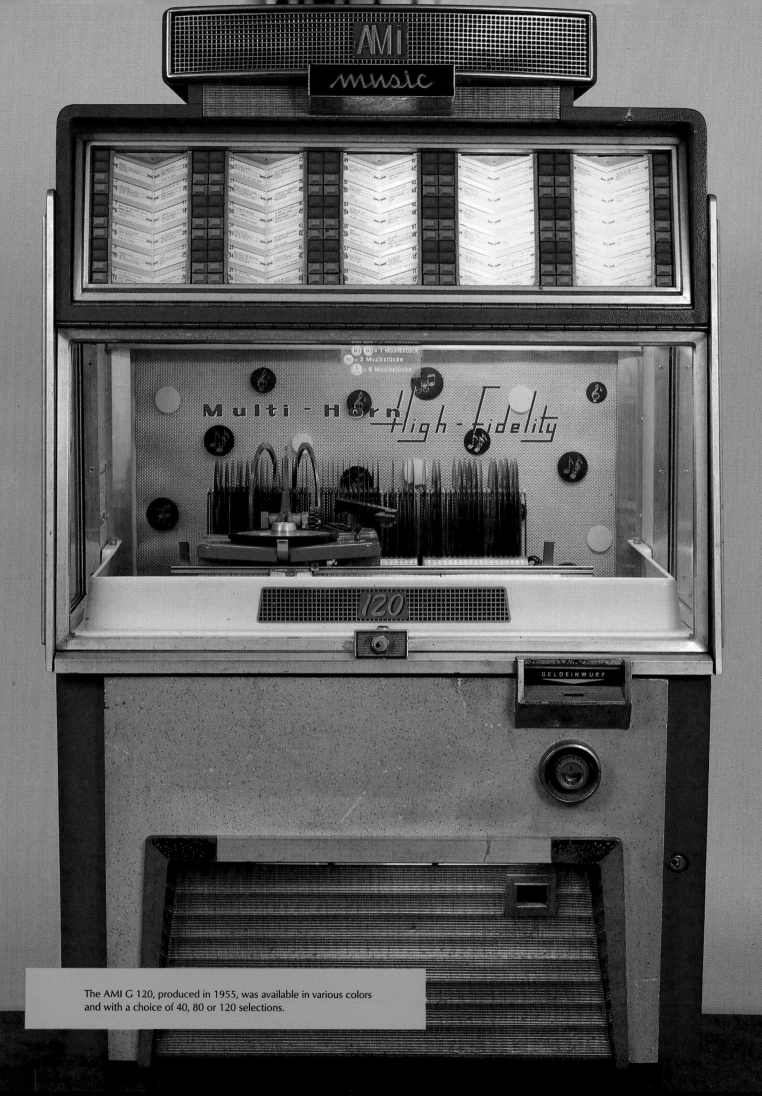

The AMI G 120, produced in 1955, was available in various colors and with a choice of 40, 80 or 120 selections.

A Wurlitzer 1900, made in 1956

Wurlitzer 2100, manufactured in 1956. The company sold 4,347 of these imposing chrome machines. The horizontal rack and vertical tone arm were a typical feature of Wurlitzer jukeboxes of the time.

A 1957 Seeburg KS 200. Despite a fanfare of publicity which proclaimed "the exciting new Seeburg 200 with super styling," the machine was in production only from March to December 1957.

AMI I 200 (1958). The design of this machine is slightly reminiscent of automobiles of the time, and offered 200 selections.

A German machine, the "Bimbo-Box," made by UTA Elektroakustik in 1958. A tape loop provided 150 titles to choose from, and the monkeys played along with the music. Aimed at children, the machine could also be fitted with Disney figures or hares.

Wurlitzer 2400 (1959). Like many jukeboxes of the 1950s and '60s, this machine had minimal lighting, and there was more emphasis on the mechanism and the record stacking system. The 2400 boasted 200 selections and stereo sound.

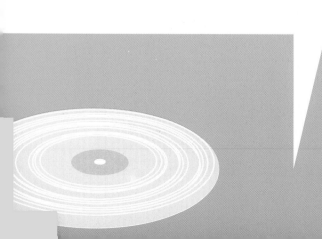

Rock-Ola "Music Vendor" (1958). This jukebox could be fixed to the wall or stood on the floor, but was not a huge success and would not win any prizes in a beauty contest.

Rock-Ola "Tempo II
Model 1478,"
a differently colored
version of the original.

Seeburg M 100 B from the early 1960s. This was the successor to the 100 A, and had 100 tracks to choose from. It was on the market for only just over a year.

Rock-Ola "Model 1496 Empress 120" from 1962, with the Rock-Ola crown on the loudspeaker grille, awaiting restoration. Its slightly rounded design seems to have been influenced by automobiles of the time.

The "Flying Petticoats" from Cologne enjoying their favorite pastime.

Seeburg DS 160 (1962). The Seeburg crown has been replaced by a "7-up" advertisement: the operator would have been in trouble if Seeburg had found out.

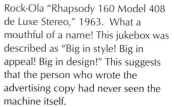

Rock-Ola "Rhapsody 160 Model 408 de Luxe Stereo," 1963. What a mouthful of a name! This jukebox was described as "Big in style! Big in appeal! Big in design!" This suggests that the person who wrote the advertising copy had never seen the machine itself.

Wurlitzer "Lyric" (1960s). The original only had two white fluorescent tubes, which I changed. A typical 1960s jukebox.

Thirty years on, the 1950s and '60s still exert a strong appeal. Here, a 1946 AMI "A" is still going strong in Dee's Diner, Düsseldorf.

Bergmann S 100 (1960s). This machine offered 100 selections and could be either wall-mounted or free-standing.

AMI "Continental," (1961), also known, for obvious reasons, as "Radar Box" and "Sputnik" and featuring 200 selections.

Wurlitzer 1050, made in 1973.
This model was an attempt to
stave off the company's
collapse, but unfortunately it,
too, proved a failure.

Rock-Ola 464 (1976) –
a late example of hippy
psychedelia from the
jukebox industry.

Dee's

JUKEBOX-BEER

More than a beer–it's a way of life!

REAL GERMAN
BEER

"Gazelle": a reproduction combining features of the Wurlitzer 850 and 950

"Peacock": also a modern reproduction

Reproduction of a Wurlitzer 71